A Picture Book of Benjamin Franklin

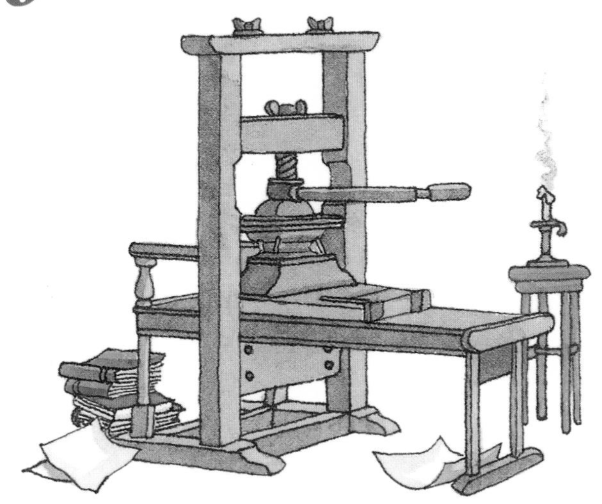

David A. Adler

illustrated by John & Alexandra Wallner

Holiday House / New York

To Johanna Hurwitz
D.A.A.

To reading and imagination
J.W. and A.W.

Printed in the United States of America

Library of Congress Cataloging-in-Publication Data

Adler, David A.
A picture book of Benjamin Franklin / written by David A. Adler :
illustrated by John and Alexandra Wallner.
p. cm.
Summary: Surveys the life of Benjamin Franklin, highlighting his
work as an inventor and statesman.
ISBN 0-8234-0792-6
1. Franklin, Benjamin, 1706-1790—Juvenile literature.
2. Statesmen—United States—Biography—Juvenile literature.
3. Printers—United States—Biography—Juvenile literature.
4. Inventors—United States—Biography—Juvenile literature.
5. Scientists—United States—Biography—Juvenile literature.
[1. Franklin, Benjamin, 1706-1790. 2. Statesmen. 3. Inventors.]
I. Wallner, John C., ill. II. Wallner, Alexandra, ill. III. Title.
E302.6.F8A28 1990
973.3'092—dc20 89-20059 CIP AC
[B] [92]
ISBN 0-8234-0792-6
ISBN 0-8234-0882-5 (pbk.)

Other books in David A. Adler's *Picture Book Biography* series

A Picture Book of George Washington
A Picture Book of Abraham Lincoln
A Picture Book of Martin Luther King, Jr.
A Picture Book of Thomas Jefferson
A Picture Book of Benjamin Franklin
A Picture Book of Helen Keller
A Picture Book of Eleanor Roosevelt
A Picture Book of Christopher Columbus
A Picture Book of John F. Kennedy
A Picture Book of Simón Bolívar
A Picture Book of Harriet Tubman
A Picture Book of Florence Nightingale
A Picture Book of Jesse Owens
A Picture Book of Anne Frank
A Picture Book of Frederick Douglass
A Picture Book of Sitting Bull
A Picture Book of Rosa Parks
A Picture Book of Robert E. Lee
A Picture Book of Sojourner Truth
A Picture Book of Jackie Robinson
A Picture Book of Paul Revere
A Picture Book of Patrick Henry

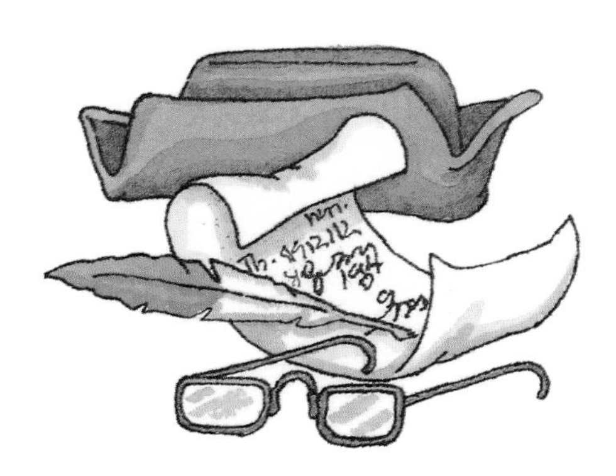

Benjamin Franklin was born in Boston, Massachusetts on January 17, 1706. Massachusetts was then one of the thirteen American colonies that belonged to England.

There were seventeen Franklin children. Benjamin's father hoped that Benjamin, the tenth and youngest son, would grow up to be a minister.

Benjamin always had lots of ideas. When he was still a young boy, he invented swimming paddles that fit over his hands and helped him swim faster.

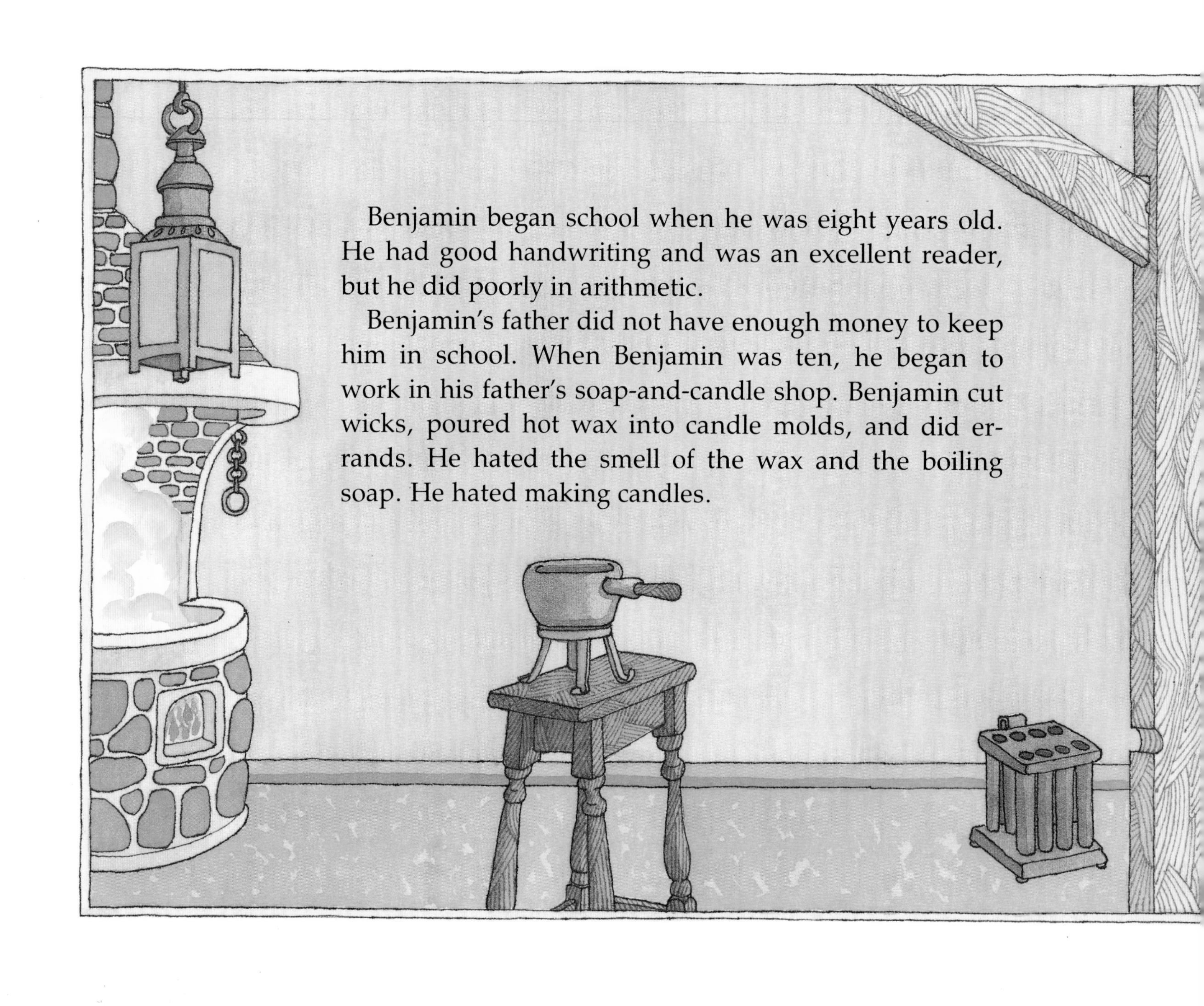

Benjamin began school when he was eight years old. He had good handwriting and was an excellent reader, but he did poorly in arithmetic.

Benjamin's father did not have enough money to keep him in school. When Benjamin was ten, he began to work in his father's soap-and-candle shop. Benjamin cut wicks, poured hot wax into candle molds, and did errands. He hated the smell of the wax and the boiling soap. He hated making candles.

Benjamin wrote poetry. He loved books and reading. So when he was twelve, his father put Benjamin to work in a print shop. The printer and owner of the shop was James Franklin, Benjamin's older brother.

James Franklin printed one of the first newspapers in America, *The New England Courant*. Benjamin set type and ran the press. He also wrote clever articles for the newspaper. He signed them *Mistress Silence Dogood* so no one would know who wrote them. James was angry when he found out that his brother was *Silence Dogood*. He refused to print any more of the articles.

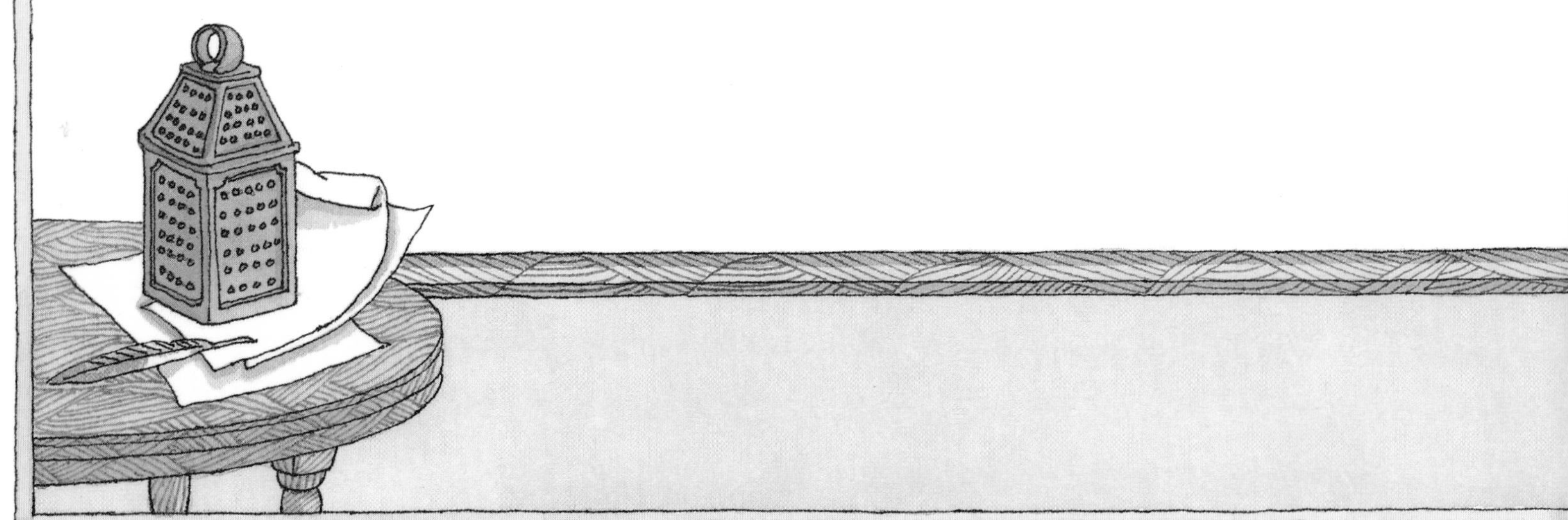

When Benjamin was seventeen, he left his brother's shop. He went to New York City and then to Philadelphia, where he worked in a print shop.

Soon after Benjamin arrived in Philadelphia, he met Deborah Read. They were married in 1730. Benjamin had three children, William, Francis, and Sarah.

In 1728, when Benjamin was twenty-two, he set up his own print shop and published a newspaper, *The Pennsylvania Gazette*. Benjamin worked hard. He became the official printer of Pennsylvania. Later he became the official printer for New Jersey, Delaware, and Maryland, too.

Once a year, beginning in 1732, Benjamin printed *Poor Richard's Almanack*. At the time, it was the most popular almanac in America. It had information on the weather, recipes, and a calendar of important dates. It also had stories and wise sayings, including "Early to bed, early to rise, makes a man healthy, wealthy, and wise" and "Haste makes waste."

Printing
Shop.

Benjamin Franklin had worked hard since he was a boy. By 1748, at the age of forty-two, he was a rich man. He retired from the printing business. He spent his time in public service, inventing and experimenting.

Benjamin Franklin helped set up Philadelphia's first fire and police departments. He helped to start the first lending library and the first hospital in America. He was made postmaster of Philadelphia and later postmaster of all thirteen American colonies.

Philadelphia
Benjamin Franklin
BENJ. FRANKLIN

Benjamin Franklin invented the Franklin stove. It saved fuel and heated a room better than a fireplace. He invented bifocal glasses and a "long arm" to reach books on high shelves. He also invented the lightning rod that saved many homes from fires.

Benjamin Franklin was very interested in electricity. In one dangerous experiment, he flew a kite in a thunderstorm. When lightning struck the kite, sparks flew from a key attached to the string. Benjamin had proved that lightning is electricity.

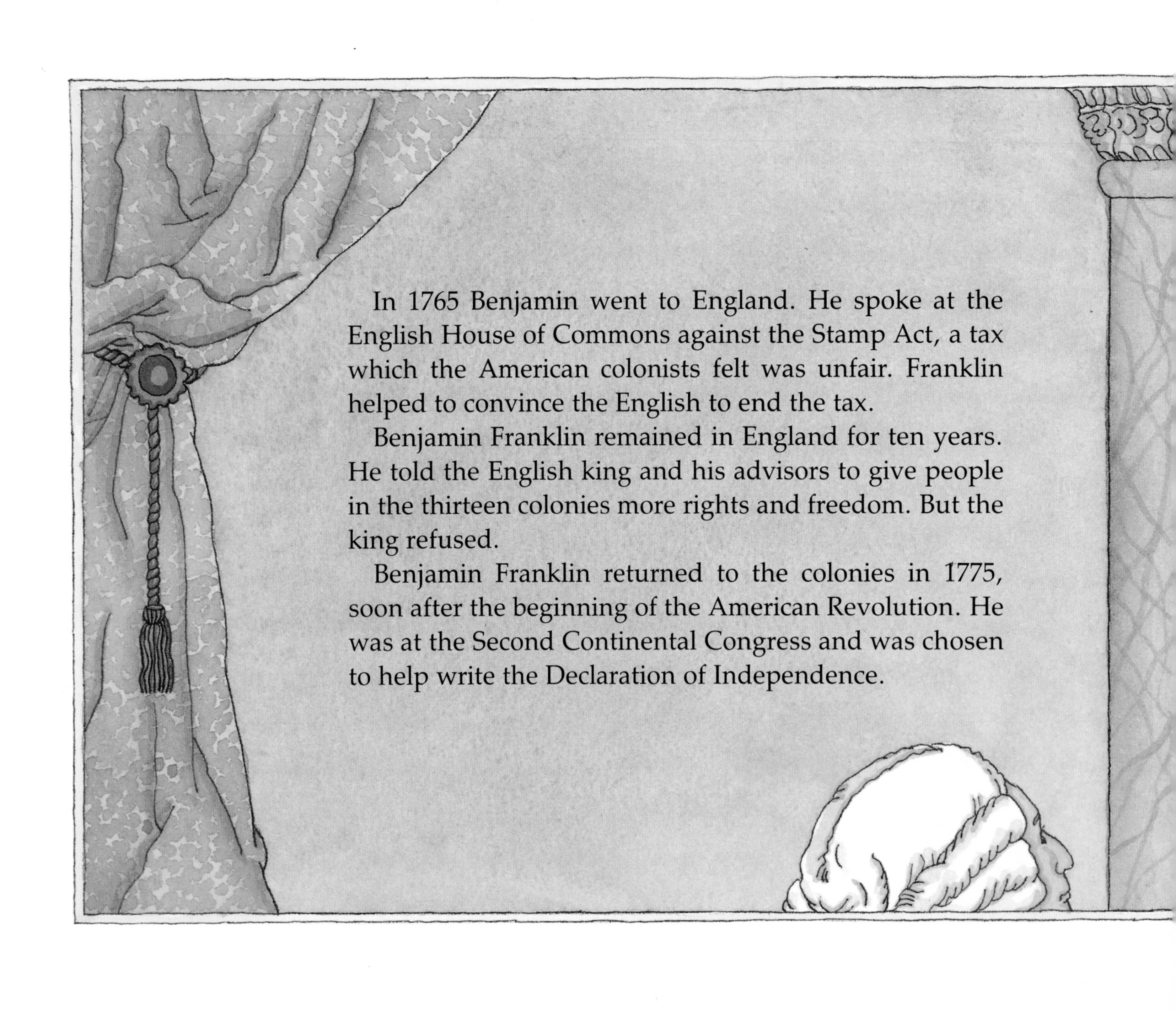

In 1765 Benjamin went to England. He spoke at the English House of Commons against the Stamp Act, a tax which the American colonists felt was unfair. Franklin helped to convince the English to end the tax.

Benjamin Franklin remained in England for ten years. He told the English king and his advisors to give people in the thirteen colonies more rights and freedom. But the king refused.

Benjamin Franklin returned to the colonies in 1775, soon after the beginning of the American Revolution. He was at the Second Continental Congress and was chosen to help write the Declaration of Independence.

In 1776 Benjamin Franklin traveled to France to ask the French people to help America in its fight for independence. The French people liked Benjamin's clever stories. They honored him as a great scientist. The French king Louis XVI agreed to send money and weapons to America.

America won its independence, and Benjamin Franklin helped write the peace treaty with England.

Benjamin Franklin returned to Philadelphia in 1785. He was an American hero. When his ship was about to dock, cannons were fired in his honor. Bells were rung, and a crowd waited to greet him.

Two years later, in 1787, a constitution was being written to govern the new United States. Benjamin Franklin was the oldest delegate to the Constitutional Convention. He was eighty-one years old.

In his final years, Benjamin Franklin wrote his autobiography. He also spoke out against slavery and worked to outlaw it.

Benjamin Franklin died on April 17, 1790 at the age of eighty-four.

When Benjamin Franklin wrote his will, he called himself "Benjamin Franklin, printer." But people all over the world knew him as more than a printer. They knew him also as a writer, scientist, inventor, and statesman. They knew him as Benjamin Franklin, great American.

IMPORTANT DATES

1706	Born on January 17 in Boston.
1718–1723	Worked in his brother's print shop.
1728	Opened his own print shop in Philadelphia.
1730	Married Deborah Read.
1732–1758	Published *Poor Richard's Almanack*.
1765–1775	Represented the American colonies in England.
1776–1785	Represented the United States in France.
1782	Helped write peace treaty with England.
1787	Delegate to the Constitutional Convention.
1790	Died on April 17 in Philadelphia.

AUTHOR'S NOTE

There are historians who question whether Benjamin Franklin actually flew a kite during a thunderstorm, but it is generally accepted that he did.

D.A.A.